TO LET THE SUN

To Let the Sun

✶

JOHN ALLEN TAYLOR

The University of Arkansas Press
Fayetteville ✶ 2025

Copyright © 2025 by John Allen Taylor. All rights reserved.

ISBN: 978-1-68226-271-9
eISBN: 978-1-61075-836-9

29 28 27 26 25   5 4 3 2 1

Manufactured in the United States of America

Designed by William Clift

♾ The paper used in this publication meets the minimum requirements of the American National Standard for Permanence of Paper for Printed Library Materials Z39.48-1984.

LIBRARY OF CONGRESS CATALOGING-IN-PUBLICATION DATA

Names: Taylor, John Allen, author.
Title: To let the sun / John Allen Taylor.
Description: Fayetteville : The University of Arkansas Press, 2025. | Series: Miller Williams poetry series
Identifiers: LCCN 2024045109 (print) | LCCN 2024045110 (ebook) ISBN 9781682262719 (paperback) | ISBN 9781610758369 (ebook)
Subjects: LCGFT: Poetry.
Classification: LCC PS3620.A946544 T6 2025 (print) | LCC PS3620.A946544 (ebook) | DDC 811/.6—dc23/eng/20241023
LC record available at https://lccn.loc.gov/2024045109
LC ebook record available at https://lccn.loc.gov/2024045110

for Marie

Contents

Series Editor's Preface   xi

Anyway   3

On the Anniversary of a Failed Suicide   4

History of My Godlessness   5

Golden Pothos   6

Monster   8

Come Sunday   9

Woe   10

Invocation   12

Already   13

Confession   15

Birdsong   16

Johnny   17

Hospital Song   18

I Keep My Kidney Stones in a Salt Shaker   19

Vicodin Thinks of Necessity   20

Vicodin Thinks of the Goldfish   21

Four Years Empty   22

Sleep Song   23

Self-Harm   24

Dear Friend   25

In the Garden   27

Letter to My Mother   28

After All   29

Elegy for a Mallard   30

Death in Late October Revisited   31

In the Middle, Again   32

The Last Bramble Cay Melomys   33

Trying to Pray   34

In Memory of the Hermit Crab Named Eugene   35

Two Moments with This Poem in Common   36

Making Bread   37

Do You Want to Have Children?   39

Amazing Grace, Etc.   41

Mother's Day   42

Sleep Hygiene Protocol   43

Horoscope with Calcium   45

Blood Song   46

Elegy for a Chicken Named Roxane   47

Sugar Ant   48

After My Therapist Tells Me to Rewrite the Nightmare   49

Wherein I Reclaim the Smells You Stole from Me   51

Unmonstrous   53

I Call My Father   54

Whole   55

Love Poem for Marie   57

The Boy Thinks of After   59

Here   60

How   62

Prayer   63

To Carry   65

Acknowledgments   67

Series Editor's Preface

Whew.

Damn. This America.

This raucous, malfunctioning, precocious, thuggish, absurdly tender, enviable, poisonous, utterly mercurial snitch of a nation. This bumptious, blustering, broken experiment. This circle of arms, haven for guns and greed, this cult of celebrity, this shelter and sanctuary, this bait for demons and demagogues. This place we call—home.

Like it or not, we're surrounded by our country. It hasn't been easy to watch its many wounds rise to the surface for anyone to see.

And maybe it's my imagination (poets are notorious for their imaginations), but I suspect more people are seeking out poetry to help with the increasingly difficult task of entering the day—screeching at Alexa to STFU, flopping out of bed, and cringing at the day's first headline.

The actual truth, assuming anyone can recognize it anymore, has been in very short supply lately. (Catch any segment of a certain cable news network for all the evidence you need.) It's not surprising that more and more neophytes are eyeing poetry's unfamiliar and untrod landscape, wondering what all the fuss has been about, also wondering if there's any semblance of truth they might stumble upon.

Longtime lovers of poetry are also on the prowl, looking for proof that they've always been savvier than everyone else, that "the truth"—in each and every one of its sneaky incarnations—has lurked in stanzas all along. Because poets are still doing what we've been doing all along—serving as unerring and resolute witnesses, calling it like we see it, and lending lyricism and light to the chaos in an attempt to make the hardest of hard truths a little easier to stomach.

Of course, there's that nagging question: *What is truth anyway?* That query has always been the nagging stuff of nightmares and—lucky us—we writers are asked more frequently than anyone else.

I believe that truth in poetry is realizing the strength of our root, as Ukrainian poet Julia Kolchinsky does here in "On the 100th day of war in my birthplace:" from her spellbinding book *Parallax*:

I am still born

> in a country named outskirt, a city
> named river, on a street named goddess
> of the hunt, born in a government-assigned
> apartment where our balcony was my preferred
> place to sleep while my papa sang
> inappropriate songs about alcoholics treating their dogs better
> than their women & a neighborhood Baba
> would shout up from the courtyard,
>
> *He's ruining the child with that language.*
>
> Now, I sing my children to sleep
> in that same mother tongue [...]

Julia, one of this year's Miller Williams runners-up, came to this country as a Jewish refugee in the early 1990s. In her poems, she clutches at a feeling of home that is both unfamiliar and deeply treasured, longs for all that was left behind, struggles to come to terms with the rampant violence devastating a landscape that still, in so many encouraging and heartbreaking ways, belongs to her.

After reading Julia's manuscript, I could only sit with its cogency, reflecting upon its fierce lyric and how an oft-told story—that of the distant daughter of a country now embroiled in war—takes on singular force. These are poems of the unsettled moment, urgent and restless, deftly crafted to illustrate how war becomes part of the migrant's body, how its sole purpose is to change what truth truly is.

In John Allen Taylor's *To Let the Sun*, another of 2025's stellar runners-up, the truth is resolute and resounding. It troubles the poems the way a bomb troubles what dares to surround it.

There is no one who lives this life unbothered. We are all, in some way, wounded. If you are a conscious human of hurtin' age, it's a given that your heart is breaking as you read this. Loved ones die, fortunes are lost and made and lost again, reputations crumble, diseases slash lifelines. Our bodies are pummeled, ignored, taken for granted, invaded. We constantly strive to fold and carve and mold ourselves toward normal.

How?

Poets write our way into the lives we envision. But first we must write into and past the wounding.

That's so much of what John is doing in *To Let the Sun*. He does so without hiding in the squeaky folds of sentiment or resorting to the tired language that latches itself to trauma. In these captivating poems, there are regrets dissected, pain tugged to the surface, love celebrated, secrets searching for voice.

Here. The opening lines of John's heartrending "Golden Pothos":

> I refuse to imagine
> a changed past, another
> childhood. *What if he*
> *never touched you?* she asks
> & I shrug into my cowardice
> *I don't know, I do not know.*
> A pothos hangs over us
> where we sit on the bed.
> The vine doesn't know summer
> rages outside the window,
> doesn't fret about the next
> watering, doesn't remember
> falling from its perch
> on the drive from Boston
> to Detroit when we moved
> last July. It remembers
> the shears, after.

If you ended that passage with a sudden intake of breath, you're not alone. I too was spurred to experience the largeness of moment through the smallness of what the poet allowed me to see. In this poem, as in so many others in *To Let the Sun*, I heard the thick thread of once-suppressed pain woven throughout the now out-loud lines. I heard the wounding, and I was spellbound as John went about his necessary work. But these are not—as we hear all too often—"poems of healing." These memories bellow and screech instead of whisper.

Once I'd made my manuscript selections and learned John's name, I spent hours reading his forays into the minefield, his crafting of truths with their tangled beginnings in the mind of a child, now splendidly wrought in the hands of a poet whose dazzling and devastating poems are his root to the world.

As John declares in "Confession,"

> Only a razor in a steady hand
> could have left this mark.

If you ended that couplet with a sudden intake of breath, you're not alone.

When normal respiration resumes, read this snippet from "Alarm," an offering in Lena Moses-Schmitt's *True Mistakes*—the third of our runners-up (these are in no particular order, by the way).

> This morning, the sound of water rushing underground.
> I don't know what this means, or where the source.
> As if I'm walking on a paved-over river. Fossilized current,
> old patterns of thought. What am I grieving?
> A few blocks away, a truck backs up,
> releasing a slow series of beeps, endless
> ellipses, and I realize it's the same
> alarm that's been going off inside me,
> distant and silent, all year.

What *are* we grieving? The truths we're forced to confront are the thousand answers to that single question. Grieving is a constant. As I'm writing this, the television in the next room blares with news of another child wielding an assault weapon, another school haunted and slapped quiet, another four lives lost. Tomorrow we will reenter the world, warily meet each other's eyes, and nod imperceptibly, acknowledging our ritual of shared terror.

Lena is who we are when we're back in our rooms alone, pummeling the mirror with questions that leave scars. After all, the first truth must be always us—and *True Mistakes* is a lyrical surface for our vulnerabilities, an admission that the human family, for all its boisterous songs and bright colors, is a family of fracture.

The tender but forthright avowals in *True Mistakes* are ones I recognize and have struggled to hear. In these poems, Lena is in frank conversation with her flawed, confounded, and tentative self, and within that revelatory dialogue lurks a truth for every reader.

And now. [FANFARE]

When you happen upon an unforgettable manuscript written by someone you have never met, you instinctively begin to formulate a picture of the poet. You assume educational backdrop, ethnicity, hometown, time spent as a poet, political leanings, creative influences, family life, etc. You can't help it. You're often wrong, sometimes you're right. But you can't help it.

I pictured someone very much like Greg Rappleye, but—and this has nothing at all to do with physical bulk—I didn't picture quite as much of him as there actually is. Not even close.

That said, there's a lot that goes into being Greg Rappleye—winner of the 2000 Brittingham Prize in Poetry, revered teacher at Hope College in Michigan, a frequent presence in the savviest lit journals, and the artist behind the most impressive manuscript in this competition. (Yes, yes, I know—*arguably*. But what the judge says goes.) He's a solid, upright, immensely talented poet who (here comes the part that threw off my conjured portrait of said poet) just happens to write nerve, sonically explosive lines like—

> But above all our American nights, this was legend—
> screams, wingéd ashtrays, shattered bottles,
> a wall splattered with blood that would copper-brown
> as a martyr's relic, holy and untouched,
> into a new millennium, the Philco and its duct-taped
> bunny ears, chucked out the door to smithereens,
> the berserk words tumbling through spittle
> flecked lips and *Looney Tunes* lipstick,
> the syllables of which we knew
> were mortal sins the nuns would drag us off
> to confess were we to chant them, in sing-song
> voices, on the whirl-around at St. Mary's School,
> until Mam was locked in the bathroom
> slashing at air with a straight-edge,
> primed to cut Da's throat, and Da outside the door
> flailing with a spike maul, shattering fat-wood
> to smoker chips, and my sister, age 8,
> came whispering to our rooms.

Uh, wow.

Barley Child goes on and on that way, full to bursting with heat and motion and sound and rampaging narrative, rich with human triumph and frailty, populated with memorable characters whose lives waste no time entering our own. I read the entire manuscript out loud, reveling in the energized unreeling of narrative, the robust characters, but most of all, the unrelenting *song* of it all.

There's no way to read *Barley Child* and not wallow in the midst of all that aural audaciousness, no way not to live within its story, no way to close the book after that last line in that last poem and not believe all of it to be true. True in the way that a poet sees truth—as a resolution for anguish, as acknowledging home, as an unswerving bond between sound and story.

Judging this year's competition was insanely difficult. They've all been. Astounding poems are everywhere, and poets continue unearthing truths when we most need them. Thanks to my stalwart screeners, who passed along the very best, you now hold the best in your hands.

PATRICIA SMITH

TO LET THE SUN

Anyway

the fungal gnats are blooming again & my mother weeps for me she says *I beg you not to...* / I catch as many flies as I can / rub them to dust / then to nothing / between my fingers / the sun sets exhausted / the moon is late / the phone grows hot against my ear I am practicing silence / I am practicing assembly / rebuilding myself atom by atom / fly by fly by fly / when I die I ask to be buried quickly / I am weary of cohesion / of introducing myself to each fly / I say *forgive me* / *like you I never expected to survive this long* / I hang up the phone & do not apologize / this is a skill I am learning / you're invited to take a walk with me / the moon will be along / I hope you'll come / though I am going anyway

On the Anniversary of a Failed Suicide

How complicated a lyric framed
by death

or not death: life as accident, life
as failure.

Tonight I drink Swiss Miss
with rum

& pet a whale-ish cat with one white paw.
How strange

to know fragility like this: a petal's
width

from holiness. Once, my grandmother
asked if I am born

again. Yes, I told her, I was.

History of My Godlessness

Small one, holding a bullfrog
in a Tennessee summer night

how well you worship & despair—
your friends around you

listening to Christian radio
& mystified beyond your reach.

Then the lightning bugs
which you only knew

from books spring up
about you, a grist of doubt

& hum. The air thick & humid
settles like moss at your throat—

you lean back onto the asphalt
& set the frog above your head

like a crown. You can't see the stars
for the thunderheads, but the bugs

descend like a righteous plague.
Your friends flee, fragments

of *holy— holy— holy—* skip
like rabbits after them. Rejoice

child, you could not have followed.
Lift your hands & receive this kingdom.

Be literal. Be devoured by light.

Golden Pothos

I refuse to imagine
a changed past, another
childhood. *What if he
never touched you?* she asks
& I shrug into my cowardice
I don't know, I do not know.
A pothos hangs over us
where we sit on the bed.
The vine doesn't know summer
rages outside the window,
doesn't fret about the next
watering, doesn't remember
falling from its perch
on the drive from Boston
to Detroit when we moved
last July. It remembers
the shears, after. But what
of them? It won't wonder
if I forget to water tomorrow
or the day following, won't
wonder even as it hangs limp
in its pot, won't wonder
as it dies, won't wonder
in death, won't wonder
as it crisps & falls onto the bed
onto our faces screwed up
by small, curious agonies.
I know I am not lost. I know
memory is a compendium
of fright. I know memory

is not healed by time, but
by the oddities
with which we adorn our lives,
the fragilities we need to know
we're needed by.

Monster

The frog moon erupts from the Atlantic
& the fish begin to sing.

I move my body through surf & imagine foam teeth
dissolve me—

this, my most precious spell. Death is a blue burglar
but I am vigilant.

I address the monster inside me, which is animal
& male: Do you remember

guiding my small hand over the quail's nest?
The stick & the squelching.

You were there at the birth of my terror—
made me follow

my hands warily: my body the first cast stone
you named manhood.

May the surf unthread you from me. May you feel
a grief that swells

like flood waters between us, so the kelp will drift
& the fish not pause

& you diminish into whichever abyss
you choose.

Come Sunday

You said Jesus would come into me,
into my heart. I remember your words,
Come back if you don't feel it—
we will try again. I came back. I came back.
I remember the pith of those years:
yellow walls, ringed with paper chains.
Chains the color of flesh: *incarnation*
you said. What use was flesh if not my own
to give away—what use was your gentleness?
Incarnation was the wooden quietness
of your pleasure, your tongue on the roof
of my mouth, the thrill of you
coming to fetch me. Jesus was a bulge
when you held me on your lap. I remember
the jealousy of those days, the come-thous,
the founts, your incarnation, the flesh-chain
reaching me through all these years.

Woe

> *to those who enact evil statutes ... what will you do in the day of punishment ... and where will you leave your wealth?*
> **ISAIAH 10:1-4**

When I was young I wanted to be
my sister, untouched

unseen by men. How wrong
I was then:

neither of us had any chance of escape
& now to wear myself

like a thin veil of mourning. My body
the same as the man's

who loomed over me—this form
a herald of woe.

                Yesterday

a New York Supreme Court justice favored
Sony over Kesha—

favored what is owed over what the body
cannot forget.

I stand naked in the mirror & assess
what remains:

power & trauma, two snakes
each desperate

to finish eating the other.
Tell me

what does it mean when flesh yields
to the abstract, yields

under the weight of what
cannot be weighed.

When the woman was brought before
Jesus to judge, he stooped

to write in the dirt. He set his body down.

Invocation

Let there not be sex. Let the tangle
in my throat come free. Let

there be hand-holding. Let there be
singing or not singing but let it be sound alone

or silence. Let me be clear: I desire you
as a body desires a body. As a fern

bends towards the window, night & day.
Let us draw near in the making of bread

in the sound of your laughter
as you watch television three rooms

away. Let there not be sweat. Let the smell
of my body be wind at high altitude, your body

salt & sand. Let a warm cheek be enough.
Let me be understood when I flinch

at touch. Let my thighs be the garden Eden,
vacant. Let the apple. Let my fingers worry

the stone smooth. Let my mouth be drought.
Let my *No* be the whisper of a knife

from its sheath. Let your patience be
repaid ten thousand times. Let love come

without hands or lips. Let the bedsheet
touch us both at once.

Already
Ecclesiastes 3 (NIV)

I've read the wisdom
of the old poet how
it comes with time
& seeing time pass
in a pretty stone gently
set atop a dresser
& not how the stone
moves & not how
the stone changes
because it does not
change it only gathers
to it the dust from
our bodies & each
day's opening tell me
what do I do with
this wisdom when
I see the small dog
white as a fall cloud
lift up the terrible
body of an SUV
how she emerges
from the tire's tread
unmarred & whole
how she walks limpless
to the sidewalk how she
lays her body down
how did the old poet
put it? *there is a time
for everything* there is
a time for pulling over
to hold the white dog

there is a time for her
to leap forward
& run there is a time
to chase a dog already
dead though it races
the twelve blocks home
where her family waits
a time to tell
what has happened
a time for mourning
before death comes
truly didn't the old poet
say *as one dies, so dies
the other* didn't they say
all have the same breath
didn't they say *everything
is meaningless* everything is
meaningless you know
as you chase the dog
block after block running
running nearly home

Confession

I don't require your belief
in my lie, just your participation.
Only a razor in a steady hand
could have left this mark.
I'm not speaking to anyone, or
to you. You who sees keloids
snake across my arms and legs.
You who sees cowardice—
who can't know how old
the scars, how young the hand.
You don't have to kiss them
or say anything at all, as I growl
myself through nakedness.
You can find your own way
to understanding. I will not speak of it.

I dreamed last night of dying
& of those who mourned
wrongly. Who called me survivor.
But a cat looks like any cat a block away.
I came into the world
bloody & I will leave it feral.

Birdsong

I step into the mirror & kiss myself
full on the mouth. When I open my eyes

we are kestrels with talons buried
in each other's chests. How beautifully

we rend each other rib from rib.
Beak sharpens beak. We stop for drinks

& tattoo ourselves on the torsos
of sleeping men. We are all John

& blood is our birthright.
What weapon can I use against myself

but my own silence sown in my flesh?
Burs & beet seed. I am a garden of wrath.

How beautiful I am, roots roiling red
from the earth. Plumed men beak

to beak. The crash of breaking glass
I take to be the sound of rain.

Johnny

This is the body, the eight-year-old body, cream-skinned, cat-boned,
    quiet.

        Call the body Johnny.

Bend the body—it will not break.
            Bend forward, Johnny.

The skull is small as a child's skull is small, but the mouth is morning
    on the seventh day.

        Open, Johnny.

Its tongue moves but makes no sound. No mother comes. No father.
    Who made this body?
           Bend over, Johnny.

Undress the body: those hands not the father's. The nails ...
    The voice lamb soft & wolfish:
                Shush, Johnny.

The body opens but does not break.
                  It has never broken.

Its hands are small. Its hands are clumsy with what they must hold.

Hospital Song

The nurses pass like wisps
of blue cloth brandishing syringes.
They say *This is for pain*
or *This is for vermillion*
or *This is for dragon.* They know
my smile means I stopped
caring days ago. Their joking
means they stopped
caring. We pass time
by almost existing. I notice
how the other patients move
their bodies through doorways,
across thresholds, testing
the air with all their skin,
their sick clothes, their capes
& veils catching the stale light.
Sometimes, they die. But I remain
with the wraiths & their jokes,
their needles & pokes that sustain me
just this side of pain,
of feeling. Suddenly
carnations & half-familiar
faces at my bedside. I say
I hate carnations & smile,
rising naked from my bed.

I Keep My Kidney Stones in a Salt Shaker

on the top shelf of my bookcase
between a guide on egg identification
& my grandfather's red Darby Bible.
A friend told me it's like a smoker keeping
cancer in a box of Winstons, which sounds
nothing like the intricate, calcified
crystals my kidneys turn out from time to time.
Snowflakes cast in stone, the color of raw
sugar, each one a different, unique pain.
They clink in the shaker when I bring
it down to make a deposit. I never look
at them, but I know they're beautiful,
tempered & porous like coral.
Sometimes I wonder if Jesus
ever had kidney stones, if his doctor
recommended drinking a six-pack in a warm tub.
I wonder if that centurion's spear tore through
years of scar tissue—if Jesus said to Thomas,
This is where they were.
But the old Darby has nothing on Jesus's kidneys.
I think if he had kidney stones he would keep them
in a salt shaker on his top shelf between
a six-pack of Fat Tire & his grandfather's
copy of Song of Songs.

Vicodin Thinks of Necessity
after Laurie Lamon

tucked itching against the breast
Vicodin seeks the mouth listens
without worry the boy's breath
too shallow for sleep
or for death thinks snowdrops
& crocus kept dry in sawdust
through fall then winter Vicodin
thinks blood the boy's veins a delta
lulls craving to sleep licks the cleft
in his spine strikes a match thinks
springtime & sprouting sweet lilac
Vicodin secret & warm
crept sideways from nowhere sets
hooks & throws nets from tomorrow
the boy stirs the boy dreams
without thought of the waking
or the language of darkness
he tries to speak wordless
in bed without sweat he hungers
for rest without Vicodin thinks of the body
riddled with stones Vicodin whispers
& whispers beside him hello

Vicodin Thinks of the Goldfish

asleep in the corner of its tank
the anacharis drifting unseen
Vicodin thinks of the boy
with his nails on the glass
panicked to tapping each hour
the fish does not move
does not open the dark of its body
the spark of its eye to the night
to the boy bent in prayer

or something like prayer Vicodin
thinks of breathing the boy
remembers to breathe lifts the fish
from its slumber to stirring
for breath for Vicodin for sleep
without panic of death the fish
startles the boy with its spasm
Vicodin flexes its grip
beckons the boy to the bottle

to sleep without sleeping the boy
thinks of sunlight of aster of ivy
thinks of a mother her hand
her shears in the phlox
the boy beckons his heart to not
slow his breath to not stop thinks
in the warm pulse of lavender
autumn the ripple of starlight
the goldfish its insignificant weight

Four Years Empty

Call it spring with cut grass
and a lack of opiates. At least
the sun is out. Still too early
for hay fever but the throat
is hungry for infection.
           What propagates
dissatisfaction like the throat.
Or the second throat hovering
like a ghost within the throat.
Six grackles explore the yard.
What's more American
than a green and gray Coleman
camp chair, a cold Diet Coke,
and an orange bottle with one
last pill. This part is just image.
The bottle is four years empty.
           Across the street,
bright yellow dandelions lift
their chins to the blade.
What was it the old saint said?
If your throat causes you
to sin, rip it out and cast it
from you. Is that how it goes?
It is better for you to lose one
part of your body than for your
whole body to go—

Sleep Song

My mind hums with color, the smell of salt water out my window. I take two Ambien as sacrament. Water, not wine. Wait for sleep. My body grows heavy. Muscles like cold clay. They pretend to move. To hold my bones as I think they should. Mouth of sand. & in my left hazel eye, a corona of wheat fields. I am heat tonight. & I remember the multitude who love me. You say get up. I say come back to bed. Let me rest my back against yours. Let's exist in these suffocating threads of gravity. Your hand on my hip. My hands reaching. We can be here for a thousand years. Not rested. Not tired. My sternum becomes stone. You bring the mallets, the chisels, the picks. Let's unearth me from myself.

Self-Harm

      When you first saw my arms & legs
you took my hand & squeezed it hard.
I am not sorry for what I've done.
Though I'm learning to romanticize
the body I was born with, treasure the stretches
of myself which have never needed care. Look,
I did not bury my razors, I put them back
in the junk drawer. I will not call this self-harm
or self-care. Though I am learning my need
for precision. You wrap your arms around
my stomach & kiss the back of my neck
as I water my African violets with a syringe
I swiped from my dentist. I ask you
if you know the woman who was healed
when she touched the edge of Jesus's cloak.
No, you say, and I say, *Me either, they both
died so long ago.*

Dear Friend
after & for Brionne Janae

today we picked up branches after
a storm & I noticed a bird's nest
among the pine cones   an old nest
an unknown bird   Marie helped me
bury it   the loss of a home is a kind
of death   we know this   & I
thought of the afternoon we met
for lunch in Bellflower   just a mile
from where your parents live
& where my mother lived   where
my grandmother lived   where
my great-grandfather lived
where I spent summers in diapers
not two blocks from where you
& your brother played in the yard
twenty-five years before we met
in Boston   this is the kind of magic
I'm interested in   how we survived
childhood nearly unharmed   an armful
of scars   a headful of nightmares
what else   some people pay to watch
nightmares   the day we buried Grandad
we cleared out his house & I found
an old suitcase full of crayons
I brought it to my mother & she smiled
for the first time that day   telling
me how he packed his suitcase each
Sunday with the colors he thought
the children at church would like most
when I tell you I wept   because this too
is a kind of magic   we buried a man
& we sold a house   but we kept

a cracked Samsonite suitcase full to burst
of crayons   I like to think
though the years don't quite work   that he
passed your house on the way
to church &   seeing you   stopped
removed his hat   opened his case   & knelt
offering a bright yellow crayon

In the Garden
for Pam

The tomato plants shy away from your shears
& the unpicked cherry tomatoes drip with blossom-
end rot. You pour more tea before perching
like a mantis, all business, over the kale, snapping leaf
after leaf into your kitchen towel, an emerald mound
growing at its center.

I enter this memory the way a child creeps
to the back of his closet, the crown of his head
brushing hems of long-unworn coats & gowns—
the sacred packed with cedar & dust into each recess,
each vacancy.

When the cancer took you, I was still writing the letter
I knew even then would be my last & I crept
back to that day in the garden, the Earl Grey
hot against my chest, watching you inspect the last
tomato plant, its stalk riven in two
from blossom to crown, each half growing
like a new lung, little cherry tomatoes ripe
in the dirt—your face breaking with joy.

Letter to My Mother

It's September & the threshold between now & then thins
as the New England sky settles into dusk. I roast chickpeas
in the oven & sit to read Wright's *Branch* again. Years ago I read you
"Autumn Begins in Martins Ferry, Ohio." It's beginning here in Boston
but I'm dressed as a cardboard robot holding your hand
across the blacktop at school in Pasadena. I can smell the worms
pancaked in the rain puddles.
                                        Why has my hand felt misshapen
in every woman's hand since yours? Oh, sit down, Freud.
The chickpeas are burning & I taste the last of the Atlantic
breezing through an open window. Even as I tuck into bed
with my book, I can sense your shape in the doorway watching
as you've always watched. The two of us silent as ever,
dying for love. I know I'm just dreaming, Mom,
but September wells & the heft of America frays between us.

After All

I call my father to tell him about a poem
I've written, just published somewhere
he might see. *It's about* _____, I say.
It's not about _____. He says he loves me.

He says *You know every now and then*
I'll cast a crown that sits poorly and rocks
on its post—so I recast it.
                        My father is a dentist.
What he means is if I worked harder
I could write happy poems.
                            He says he loves
the poem I wrote for my mother.
He says *It shines*. He doesn't say that.
He says he likes how he feels
when he reads it. He means *Can you write*

about me like that?

Elegy for a Mallard

I wonder what it would take to use my body
to keep you warm like those two mallards
left in a cardboard box on my doorstep.

I told you of this, years ago, seeing them
for the first time in their makeshift cave,
freezing, a dark cloister of emerald.

Their bodies one in abandonment.

When I heard of your suicide
I drank nothing but Red Rose black tea for two weeks.
My skin has fit funny ever since.

Last spring I took the mallards to Riverfront Park
& opened the door to their borrowed dog kennel.
The two birds split like a magnet broken in two:

One for the river & the other into the grill
of a Mack semi.
                I'm sorry.
I didn't know how to warn you.

When the traffic cleared I collected the bird
& buried it in the silt
& watched its mate search for days.

We'll both wait. We're patient, you know.

Death in Late October Revisited

The fawn didn't understand steel & glass at forty-five miles an hour even to the point of impact. Even after glass & light shattered within its rib cage & moths half disintegrated smote into dust between the grill & skull. No hunt. Only the road & darkness.

    The fawn lay on its ruined side in the gutter, still walking. Hooves hooving at nothing. *Where is my breath?* How could the fawn understand Roy Orbison crooning from the radio or the man shaking above her or the rock in his white-knuckled fist poised forever above her one good eye?

In the Middle, Again

Peat moss in fingernails, vermiculite
in teeth, damselflies mount on my forearm.
What follows this, more of my life?
I carry my longing like oyster mushrooms
flared out between ribs. A shovel
in my left hand. The mailwoman knocks
and sets something in bubble wrap
on the stoop. I straighten up, swallowing
back everything I might have said.

The Last Bramble Cay Melomys

The morning paper tells us the earth is warming & the last Bramble Cay melomys has drowned in the rising sea. What did the mouse-like skitterer dream in her waning sleep? In what dried grass, woven warm & close, did the sea bear her away?

✳ ✳ ✳

On the walk from Porter Square to whichever apartment would receive her, a woman stoops to lift from the gutter a bent cattail, waterlogged & weary. She shakes it gently & tucks it upright behind another stalk before she disappears into the night of Cherry Street.

✳ ✳ ✳

When I was young, among the foothills of Los Angeles, I wandered steaming streets in first rain with a Maglite swiped from my father's car, searching for small frogs trying to cross the road. I would help them cross the road.

✳ ✳ ✳

The trash collector comes & seems to come again the next day. Three weeks later I see the same woman pause briefly before what may be the dried husk of her cattail, chittering against the concrete in the breeze. I don't know. Perhaps she didn't even pause. What use is there in this?

Trying to Pray
after James Wright

My body wanes and swells. I try
to be gracious.
A robin outcompetes a grackle
for a grub. My neighbor Dale offers
a plastic recliner, hauls it
over the fence.
In Lansing, a group of armed men
in camo from Harry's Army Surplus
swarm the capitol. I dig
a small bed for spring onions.
Dale comes to the fence, his hands
full of papery sets.
My email dings. Here I am
on my knees.

In Memory of the Hermit Crab Named Eugene
    for Allie

I've been in this pet store two hours
& can't stop thinking about
the night you went to get *Matilda*
from Blockbuster but came back
with a hermit crab named Eugene
& offered no explanation but knew
I knew an ornery hermit crab
is better than *Matilda*
which is why he stayed with me
when you traveled for Thanksgiving
& remained with me
even after you returned & why
we went to buy Eugene a companion
named Eustace but I never told you
about the night I came home to find
two whorled crabs on my keyboard
& an infinite scroll of scantily clad
crustaceans on the screen & that night
the music they made was so beautiful
it was impossible to listen
& I climbed past the coats in the closet
like I did when I was a child & frightened
with two conch shells sealed around my ears
loosed only under my mother's cool hands
but I never got to thank you so thank you
for Eugene & for the small scars he gave
when I held him too long & for your grief
when he died while I was traveling for Christmas
& the timid crab you coaxed into his old shell
without telling me but knowing I'd know
& I did know.

Two Moments with This Poem in Common

I.
After you hang up, I close the blinds
& a centipede falls from the molding
just past the tip of my nose.
Of course, it vanishes.

I walk to the bathroom for a bottle of red nail polish
& paint all twenty nails as fast as I can.

There is no way to forget your terror.

II.
Like a magician, you ask for silence
before your last act.

I watch in practiced awe as you disappear before me.
The sun settles into the Pacific & I pass
through you to a western window.

Listen I whisper & do not turn as the crickets
begin their first & final song.

Making Bread

My mother calls to apologize
for not yet making a loaf
of bread with the starter
I gave her. We pour
ourselves wine & I light
a candle called Basil & Moss
though it smells like apples
fallen onto wet autumn leaves
slowly beginning to ferment.
My mother asks how often
she'll have to feed the starter.
It depends on the temperature
I say & realize I'm being
withholding, how easy
it is not to speak. I am
in the fourteenth hour
of the loaf I mean to eat
tomorrow with friends
& in these fourteen hours
I have not needed to speak.
My mother has trouble
discerning the starter
from the splinter, the mother
from the offspring. I say
*Name the mother & you will
not lose her.* She listens
to the fridge open & close.
She listens to the dough
fall from its cane basket
onto the parchment. Listens
to the knife's quick slash
the gasp of steam the clatter

of iron on iron. My mother
asks how long it will be
in the oven. *The yeast has
eight minutes to live* I say. *If
I've timed it right, it will die
precisely when it has nothing
left to give.* She says that sounds
rather dramatic & I agree.
My mother hears my partner
enter our home & says she
can't talk anymore. I have
to go, I have to go, she says.
*Wait a moment longer. You
can hear the bread crackle & sing
when it comes out of the oven. Wait
a moment longer.* I have to go.
You know I have to go.

Do You Want to Have Children?

You see a playground I see a target

You see a school bus

You see a campsite I see a risk

You see a tent

You see a bathroom I see

You see a stall

You see a father a son I see a question

You see a Sunday school

A church I see a hunting ground

I see a pastor You see me flinch

You see a pastor I see

I see the pastor You see the child I am still

The child you see I am each muscle taut You see

I see the child the prey

Do you see Do you see the pastor

To dust we all go He speaks with his hands

We are ghosts I say with my hands

But no one has died You say no one is dead

I motion I see the hunt

Amazing Grace, Etc.
for sal

A man just walked past my office with a t-shirt that read *WAITING 4 THE RAPTURE* & I thought of you & me waiting for the train at Park Station those cold nights we stood with our backs to the wind—you waiting for the train to Braintree & me for the train north across the river. It wasn't the Rapture, I know. But do you remember how often we nearly talked about the God we pretended to know? How difficult it was to say *grace* or *faith* without flinching? How our church was four walls & a roof to house the monsters of childhood. How our church looked the other way. How our church kept small rooms of children repeating in rote the spell of their dissolution. How our church held our heads under during baptism. Outside my office window the shield bugs are collecting like a plague in the late Michigan fall & you are teaching first-year composition a thousand miles to the east & the student sitting across from me is asking for help on their essay about John Newton & the only way I can mouth the word *grace* without irony or shock is to imagine you sitting beside me in that room full of people handling our poems as priests handle confessions. I want you to know I still have the little succulent you left for me that week I watched your cats. A "silver star" *graptoveria*. It's three years old, now. Can you believe it?

Mother's Day

There is much yet to lose
Echinacea huddles beneath
wind and rain in the planter off the porch
Water pools on the sill
Two mourning doves I feed in good weather
ruffle within the viburnum
My mother calls

Quiet house on a quiet street
My voice begins
It is important to discuss the differences
between the weather here and there
Gently ask after the trumpet vine
if it continues as it has

This cannot be surrendered
A tinny voice of rain in the gutter repeats
This cannot be saved

A red pickup truck ambles up the street
through rainwater running brightly down
Someone in each dim house
waits to say goodbye

Sleep Hygiene Protocol

rewritten: *Emotion Regulation Worksheet 14b; p. 307*[1]

1. Develop & follow a consistent sleep schedule even on weekends.

2. Do not use your bed in the daytime. Do not think of your bed in the daytime.
   Strip the bed & wash the linen each day.
   Strip the bed & hide the linen each day.

3. Avoid caffeine, nicotine, alcohol, heavy meals, heavy cream, heavy metals,
   heaviness of all kinds. Avoid sharp objects or objects. Avoid linen.

4. Give yourself an hour to fall asleep. Strip the bed. Hide the bed. Gather the cat,
   a pillow & all your James Wright. Get into the bathtub. Give yourself an hour to fall asleep. Repeat.

5. DO NOT CATASTROPHIZE. Regather the cat. Walk to the corner store to say hello to Steven.
   Steven is awake & productive.
   Steven is okay.
   The cat is okay. Return home.

6. Write a love poem to Marie. Burn the bed.

---

1. Linehan, Marsha. *DBT Skills Training: Handouts and Worksheets.* 2nd ed., The Guilford Press, 2015.

7. Forget the bed—its damp & its memory. Roll out the yoga mat & practice corpse pose.
Regather beneath the cat.

8. Be still. Thrushes gather at the sill & tell you the weather.
Write a bird poem.

9. Outside, the city buses begin to creep along their routes. Write a list poem.
Give your poems to the bed pyre.
Throw your clothes on the bed pyre. Forget the bed beside you—its cunning & crush.
Regather the cat. Regather beneath the cat,
beside the pyre you must forget, beside the pyre you must forget.

Horoscope with Calcium

Mourn the evening, but do not speak of it. The moon will orbit

    what has calcified within you, what you quelled & mistook

        for dream. Don't grimace:

                you have earned

    what happens in the starlessness. Begin once more a prayer

        to whatever is unnamed.

Practice your isolation with care. Lay the razor on the soft

    of your forearm, across each pale ridge.

This night will be difficult for you—peel it open with your teeth.

                Set the razor aside

unused.

        Some will tell you to call this courage.

                It is not.

    Adorn yourself with kidney stones & bramble.   Sing.

                This is drama

    & this is clemency.

Blood Song

My loneliness solved
imagining God cut

too. Our confusion,
our soft violence.

The Mississippi
in one hand.

Our loneliness erased
by its endless flaying:

iron ore & clay
crimsoning the banks

gaped wide. Watch
the slow unearthing,

the warm ache. This is
our communion, you & I.

If you give me a river
I'll give you a blade.

Elegy for a Chicken Named Roxane

the day spins cloudless
a slight sun creeping west
over a fringe copse of tamaracks
& ponderosa pines the chicken lies
half-eaten on the potting bench
too early for flies the man sets
his back against the fence opens
a grocery bag for what remains
oyster shell grit copper feathers
on gray straw three fragments
of a last blue egg the man
wrestles with the hose
says nothing as he works
says nothing to the chicken
to the arthritis in his knees
to his silent God says nothing
to the knapweed to the pines
their laughter in the wind
their hush & chuckle he hears
the pop of a screen door
garbage pail the bright crush
of morning a pearled beak
pressed between his lips

Sugar Ant

I am 26 years old & I think my mother is very beautiful.
I always have. To be fair, I think my father is very handsome.
Sometimes, I'll show a photo to a friend, very rarely, when I trust
them to understand. I think my parents are beautiful:
My father with his soft eyes. My mother with her cool hands.
My father's broad, square hands, always dry & warm when mine
are clammy. My mother tall. Shorter than I am now, but tall.
My father short, though still taller than I am. The smell of sawdust.
The smell of peat moss. When they kiss, a kiss
practiced over 30 years, my father's eyes wrinkle above a child's smile
& he turns to me *I am so happy* & my mother blushes *I am so happy*.
I am sitting on my porch in Michigan, 2,241 miles from California,
where my parents live, & I'm watching a small ant, smaller than usual,
like three specks of pepper in costume, walk to the tip
of a sycamore leaf, six feet off the ground, 20 feet from the trunk,
sailing in a warm breeze. How have you come to be here, ant?
Where did you think you were going? Where are your parents
& their beautiful faces? Do you still believe
in righteousness? If you remembered the way home, would you go?

After My Therapist Tells Me to Rewrite the Nightmare

                    My gardening poems
turn into kidney stone poems & each time
I feign surprise. This is how we harbor
what is unreconciled.

                      My love poems
sound like rape poems—
like the nightmare returning each night.

A friend says she likes the ambiguity.
I don't like the ambiguity.

✳ ✳ ✳

In the dream, I am the man
watching me in a group of boys.

I take my hand & lead me somewhere dark—   No.

                      Make it light.

The sun is out & I am gripping my small hand.
The bed creaks beneath— No.

The bed of pine needles
beneath our bare feet pokes through calluses.
Pine cones nip at our toes.

                      I sit under a larch
& I pull me onto my lap.
                    Now what.

✳ ✳ ✳

Remember the Little Debbie Pecan Spinwheels?
My mother put one in my school lunch on my birthday.

The string cheese I ate in three bites.
But these little spirals of cinnamon & sugar & crumbles of pecan
I unraveled with such care.

✳ ✳ ✳

At the end of the nightmare there is terror.
                              I unbutton—   No.

At the end of the nightmare I am my mother

                    unwrapping a Little Debbie Spinwheel
                    to place in her boy's outstretched hand.

Wherein I Reclaim the Smells You Stole from Me

i. balsam

>>resin of heart wood & owl
song whipped up from roots
packed like casks of the scotch
you drank each night & some nights
too much when you found me beneath
you saying *please no* with balsam & reek
in my nose resin of heart wood be stripped
from me like my clothes & breath & rest
in the unlit hours resin of frankincense
& myrrh your hands at my throat be
scorched from me resin of heart
wood return on the cold wind
return to me stranger

ii. camphor

>>your body is sixty percent water   my body

>>>is sixty percent bone

>>can you hear me above the hiss in the camphor tree

>>>>each branch hanging as if laden

>>>with grapes   or each branch hanging

>>like a lung shuddering   with need

>>>>alveoli leaves

>>curdled sky   how should I breathe

iii. talcum

powder thick in the room each morning you dressed without bathing / dressed in a cloud of dust / to dust we all go with this reek in our nose / *be quiet* you said / testing the weight of your speech in my ear / my fear a weapon you wield / did wield / once wielded / once wielded / what fear / can you feel the wind rising / against your souring breath / what powder remains on the body / could remain on the body / how could you remain before me / this gale you've made me / this gale I've made me / this gale you will not withstand

Unmonstrous

Are you satisfied to know I outgrew my despair?
Do you believe it?
     Now that the scars on my arms
have settled & the cortisone shots quieted
the roiling blood. Now
that I can speak

your name aloud?
      Now, Peter.

Are you vindicated by my survival?
I was a stranger to you, an unblinking
child for you.
     Your silent Sunday saint.

Would you instead hand me this poem

& smile—would you leave me
untouched?

Tell me,
     would you pray for us
now that you're reassured—
how blessed your restraint
       how broken & sinful
this world, how unmonstrous you are?

Hold my rage a moment. Now,
stranger, you know.

I Call My Father

Who answers by telling a story
of two chipmunks & the bodies they left behind

after the neighbor's cat scared them to death.
You know, he says, I realize I've held

few pains as close as those two dead
chipmunks: the first great guilt of my life.

How teeth press their way into the dark
from the dark.

He breathes into the receiver.
How was work, we say. He says, I cast

a crown too tight, too perfect, & it snicked
over the patient's tooth. Stuck.

Couldn't get it off. What happened, I said.
If the fright is bigger than the heart, the heart bursts.

What happened, I said. Oh, I had the patient
bite down on a Jujube

I got at the gas station. When she opened
her jaw it popped right off. How's the weather,

we say. He says, When it's raining here
I suppose it must be raining there, too.

Whole
for Savannah

I can't tell you what it meant to find
my grandfather's 9mm in his sock drawer
ten weeks after the pills failed.
I emptied the magazine & chamber
as my father taught me. I checked it
three times before I pressed the muzzle
to my temple & closed my eyes.
All of the terror, none of the risk.
Call this progress.
                 When I was young
my mother used to kiss the top
of my head, where my hair leapt out
in a magnificent swirl. It still leaps
& Marie bends to kiss me there
when I sit at my desk or linger
at the dinner table.
               How might I
catalog the impulse to unmake
what my mother paid in blood
to make?
         When you came across
the text where I asked if you had ever
thought of suicide, eighteen months
after you learned of my attempt,
you looked up at me with a guilt
I could not catalog, a guilt I am
each day desperate to keep
from my mother.
              Today we talk
on the phone for just a few minutes—
you show me a video of Lisbon
out your window & I show you

the philodendron I'm repotting now
that it's March.   You don't question
my safety. We hang up loving one another
across continents, knowing we'll see
each other someday, whole,
with the beautiful crowns of our heads
still beautiful, still leaping. Hair
in wind, hair in Michigan,
hair in Portugal, hair beneath a mother's
lips, hair of one who has learned
to fall in love with the gentle swirl
of his own scalp. This morning I stand
once again in ritual & use two mirrors
to see the comb's careful work:
the top of my head is very beautiful.

Love Poem for Marie

Today Marie untangles nightmares from my hair.

Today we agree the housefly should be relocated outside & given water.

Today Marie & I decide we want blood in the poem.

Today we walk to Frank's Diner & wait for hash browns as though for a corpse flower's last bloom.

We don't look away.

Today we drink sangria from mason jars with a woman whose last name is Holliday.

Today Marie & I get lost in the stacks at Hatcher Graduate Library. We're tickled to be so lost.

Today we read Keith Taylor's poems & recite them quietly to one another.

Today a mammoth & two mastodons gaze down at us in the Museum of Natural History.

Today Marie tries to convince me mastodons are "better."

Today I hold Marie's hand while she holds a Jane Kenyon poem in her other hand.

Today Marie tells me she loves me & seems more startled than usual.

This is because of the mastodons.

Today Marie & I drink a beer brewed by Trappist monks.

Today Marie & I discuss my embarrassment at being caught staring at a bikini-clad UFC woman while drinking beer brewed by Trappist monks.

Today I am briefly chagrined.

Today I kiss her knuckles & we lumber home like mammoths.

Today we write love poems without conclusions.

Today why would we bother.

The Boy Thinks of After

unravels his muscles
hums into their sting
& dreams in the sunlight
now that it's come
now that he's passed
the night leans into the empty
beyond the bed beyond
the wrinkle & sop
of clogged pores of a throat
swollen with breath
the boy sings his body
back from the man
lingering before him
as he opens his eyes
the hands on his thighs
are his own the boy
thinks of the itch of sleep
without risk of not waking
pulls each bare leg into the light
the boy watches the trees
out the window the wind
in the trees the bright room
a corn snake enters the garden
the two of them under the sun

Here
for Brionne & Kyle

here we are   sitting in this red velvet lung
of a bar sipping martinis & asking for extra olives

our six knees knocking together like the night's
percussion   & though we're not in love

we can pretend for one evening that we'll wake
together   our throats opening & closing

out of rhythm like fish in a torn net
one of us slips through first   then another

the bed lies empty as usual & our hands
stretch back into being unheld

here we are slipping gracelessly
into the steel bodies of taxis & airplanes

thrumming a catastrophe of city & grit
into the space between us

here we are singing into our own showers
with bars of soap & dead sea creatures

into the splendid fogs of morning
 & lateness   I can't tell you how afraid

I am   how the time collects like coins
stacked on the eyes I try to open daily

now here I am eating stale airline
 peanuts   & putting away the mower

come & see the garden   the sweet peas
are spent but the squash is wild & cheerful

come & look   the sunflowers sway
like a children's choir, chickadees preening

their seedy faces   come & see the garden
come & see   it's not so terrible to exist

How

Today I'm your age when you first saw my careful chin,
my freckles in your Sunday school class,
when you took my hand from my father's, tickled me.
Did I laugh then
as you promised me your salvation?
Can you believe I still feel your fingers sear
the soft of my thigh when I sit in class, in church.
Do you believe I still go to church?
I'm sitting in bed where a woman has chosen to sleep
beside me, whom I've told I'm slow to kindle
within me what I would not have burn
so close to what you left.
Do you see her temple
rest against my leg? Listen, how cavernous
her breath, how vast we are,
how little room for anything else.
Watch how she touches me, the nail of her little finger
brushing my thigh.
How she absolves me of your sin.
Soon I'll wake her. Soon her hands. Her lips.
I woke to write a bitter poem, but look, Peter, look where I am.

Prayer

My God my mother
knows I do not

believe as a child
is meant

to believe. This
child praises

only what he may
hold: tomatoes

crushed leaves
a robin

fallen from its nest.
This child

doubts the promise
of sun

when the night is
& is

& is endless. Mother
forgive me

for I have raged
against

my temple in the night
forgive me

hymns I've rewritten
prayers offered

to an idol of the flowers
you always

kept close: nasturtium
hydrangea aster.

Oh Lord is faith
fury

or a bouquet of poppies
left to rot

on the windowsill? I
believe

if I wake I will wake
to the sound

of my mother
weeping

& her voice
calling

through the heavy stone
come forth, child

& for her Lord
I would.

To Carry

to burden oneself

to refuse to unburden oneself

to walk the warm loaf to the neighbor's door
                                      to knock
        to lift the wrapped package a few inches when the door opens

to hear *John, are you still with me?* & to not be

to learn to unburden oneself
                to watch the light dash back & forth across the black box
                          do you understand?

to light each candle each candle in the house to light them all

to *Are you awake right now?*

to hold one brown egg

to lift the dog too heavy to lift back over his fence
                to fall over the fence after

to answer the phone before looking

to stand beside Monet's *Grainstack at Sunset* holding
                a tray of champagne while a woman wearing pearls
                          reaches down your pants

to not drop the champagne

to still hear the glass rattle
                                    do you understand?

to move to not become still

to feel the strain of each locked lock
       to sleep only after

to lift each night the white sheet up to her chin
                                  to kiss her chin

to let the sun

Acknowledgments

Unending gratitude to Patricia Smith—for choosing this book and for writing poetry that continues to influence and guide my own work. Enormous thanks to David Scott Cunningham, David Manuel Cajias Calvet, Janet Foxman, Charlie Shields, William Clift, Meagan Bonnell, and everyone else at the University of Arkansas Press.

This book would not exist without my friends: Leslie Sainz, Breezy Janae, sal burnette, Kyle Dacuyan, Erin Jones, and Rage Hezekiah. My teachers and mentors: Thom Caraway, Laurie Lamon, Marilee Malott, and John Skoyles. My students.

These poems exist through the support of KMA Sullivan and YesYes Books, and Justin Rigamonti and the Carolyn Moore Writers House.

All my love to my family: Mom, Dad, Meggs, Em, Nammy, and Papa.

To Sabriel, Birdie, and Cricket.

To my whole world, Marie.

✳✳✳

Gratitude to the editors and journals that first published these poems: *Birdfeast* – "Blood Song"; *Booth* – "I Keep My Kidney Stones in a Salt Shaker"; *The Common* – "History of My Godlessness," "How," and "Johnny"; *The Cresset* – "Death in Late October Revisited"; *December* – "Self-Harm" and "Sugar Ant"; *DIAGRAM* – "Anyway"; *Dialogist* – "Come Sunday"; *Diode* – "Dear Friend" and "The Boy Thinks of After"; *Faultline* – "In Memory of the Hermit Crab Named Eugene"; *Foundry* – "Elegy for a Mallard"; *Hobart* – "Horoscope with Calcium," "Love Poem for Marie," and "Sleep Hygiene Protocol"; *Image* – "Invocation"; *The Journal* – "On the Anniversary of a Failed Suicide"; *Muzzle Magazine* – "Birdsong"; *Pleiades* – "Unmonstrous" (as "Confession, Revisited"); *Poetry Northwest* – "Already"; *RHINO* – "Monster"; *Salamander* – "Hospital Song"; *Sixth Finch* – "Making Bread"; *The Shallow Ends* – "Here"; *Split Lip Magazine* – "After My Therapist Tells Me to Rewrite the Nightmare"; *WILDNESS* – "Sleep Song"; and *Zone 3* – "In the Garden" and "I Call My Father."

Gratitude also to YesYes Books, which published many of the poems here as part of my chapbook, *Unmonstrous* (2019).